TABLE OF CONTENTS

P9-DDH-738

ACKNOWLEDGMENTS

I'd like to thank the following individuals who shared their knowledge of Bay Area cottages and who were instrumental in helping locate many of the cottages included here.

Dennis Bayer
Thomas J. Caulfield, architect
Jane Cryan, founder, The Society for the Preservation and Appreciation of San Francisco Refugee Shacks
Herb Lilly, Triumph Realty
Glenn Lym, architect
George Stewart
Jan Alff Wiegel, Zel Realty

For the generous loan of Nikon photographic equipment which was used throughout this project, I'd like to thank **Mike Phillips** and **Nikon Professional Services.**

For assistance with the photography in this project, I'd like to thank **Vince Valdes,** who participated through the Academy of Art College internship program.

I'd like to thank **Sally Woodbridge** who in addition to writing the book's introduction offered much advice and encouragement throughout the project. Additionally, I'd like to thank **Donald MacDonald** for contributing a thoughtful essay to the book and **Jeremy Kotas** for consenting to a lengthy interview which yielded much valuable information.

Finally, I'd like to thank all those cottage dwellers I did not have the opportunity to meet personally whose homes have been included here.

The following individuals were kind enough to allow me to photograph their homes. Their cooperation and enthusiasm for this project was, needless to say, vital to its completion.

Marianne Agnew
Richard L. Andrews, M.D.
Bill Bailey
David Bartlett and **Julie Devine**
Dennis and **Aggie Bayer**
Tim and **Pat Boddy**
Ted and **Mary Barone**
Colleen Butler and **Michael Burt**
Mark and **Jo Ann Coleman**
R. Leslie Dugan
Jane and **John Edginton**
Stephen and **Nancy Frisch**
Stephen Goldstine and **Emily Keeler**
Ginger Harmon
Mr. and **Mrs. M. Lambert**
Jacomena Maybeck
E. Andrew McKinney
Ruth Potter
Presidio Army Museum
Dana Rich
Raymond and **Kay Roberts**
Lou and **Lori Scalise**
Audrey Sherlock
James Stockton
Fumio and **Mieko Wada**
Nina Wehrer
Sheila Woo and **Dawn Christensen,** collectors

Bay Area Architecture has been the subject of countless books and articles over the years. From the "painted lady" Victorians to the Bay Region styles developed by the likes of Maybeck, Polk, and Wurster, the subject has been well covered. However, the humble cottage—born of a haphazard response to a complex topography and cataclysmic events such as the Gold Rush and the great earthquake of 1906—is a unique element of Bay Area architecture. As significant as any other type of Bay Area house are the hillside "dingbats," refugee shacks, Italianate "doll-houses," California bungalows, "Hansel and Gretel" cottages of the East Bay and the "simple homes" that manifest the principles of Keeler and Berkeley's Hillside Club. These modest structures are vital to the ambience of the Bay Area. Their dramatic settings—nestled under redwood and euclapytus, on secluded pedestrian streets, in well-tended gardens behind "main" houses, or on winding streets combing the hillsides—add to their mystique and charm. It is exciting—to me at least—to see a residence such as the Mathewson house in the Berkeley hills, one of Bernard Maybeck's most respected houses, juxtaposed with a backyard dingbat built by an anonymous carpenter working from plans existing only in his head. Though their respective architectural merits represent polar extremes, their shared simplicity of form, rustic charm, and delicate sensitivity to site justifies their coexistence and mutual admiration. And they have both influenced contemporary architects seeking new design solutions for the Bay Area's housing needs.

More than anything else, a cottage is a layman's term of endearment to describe a particular sort of house. Webster's Dictionary defines *cottage* as a small house, usually of one story. Dictionary definitions, though frequently lacking in nuance, are at least tidy. However, not all small houses are cottages and not all cottages are necessarily all that small. Rusticity, informality of layout, incorporation of arts and crafts elements, and a special site are at least as important as scale. The cottages included in this book range from 140 to around 1500 square feet. While the larger sized cottages are, from a contemporary perspective, frequently thought of as ample houses, they have attained their size by appropriating the attic, frequently the basement, and every other nook and cranny available. From the outside, they look as modestly proportioned as one would expect cottages to be. I have diverged equally at the other extreme by including hovels so small and meager that many would describe them as shacks or shanties rather than cottages.

I have tried to make this undertaking as definitive a document of cottage life in the Bay Area as a relatively small book can be. With thousands of cottages sprinkled throughout the Bay Area, it is regrettable that so few are included and so many left out. Despite their de facto exclusion, this document is an important one. Even with the strong local preservationist attitude, it is a foregone conclusion that many of our cottages and cottage neighborhoods, such as the Filbert Steps, are destined to have a shorter lifespan than virtually all other local architectural landmarks. The reasons are simple. Many nineteenth and early twentieth century cottages are much less substantial than most other housing and in many cases were never intended to last as long as they have already. Restoration or renovation can be nearly impossible unless one has tens or even hundreds of thousands of dollars to meet current building codes with their rigorous seismic requirements. It is difficult to imagine that after the next big quake the Filbert Steps and the cottages they access would be rebuilt to look the way they do today or that the twisted and disjointed streets of Bernal Heights lined with their weathered little dingbats would be carefully recreated to match their present ambience. It's a pity, because these are the only remnants left that evoke San Francisco, the mid-nineteenth century boom town whose shanty-covered hillsides and gulches housed hopeful adventurers seeking their fortune.

Though some significant architects' and interior designers' work is represented, this project is not intended to be a showcase of architecture or interior decorating. More important is to show what cottage living is really like. All houses affect the way we live our lives and this is particularly true of cottages. As anyone who has ever lived in a cottage will attest, there is something about them—their intimacy, coziness, or maybe their unabashed goofiness—that enraptures their occupants in a special way. It is this special magic that I've tried to capture in photographs. Because this is genuinely what cottage living is all about.

Richard Sexton

INTRODUCTION

Cottage life is one of those simple terms with complex associations. Although the cottage is defined as a house that is small and not costly, a small cheap house is not necessarily a cottage. Huts, shacks, and hovels, are all small, mean shelters lacking the qualities of snugness and coziness associated with the term *cottage.* But how big a house can be and still be small, or how much it can cost and still be a bargain are questions with variable answers depending on the time and place of the inquiry. Although Americans consider England the source of this dwelling type, the origin of the term *cottage* is the ancient Anglo-French word *cote,* also used in combination with other words like *dove* and *sheep* to describe small shelters for birds and animals. A cottage was originally a small rural shelter for peasants, a thatched hut, inconvenient and utterly lacking in amenities.

Times change. The cottage acquired a higher status in this country when the industrialization and urbanization processes of the nineteenth century changed the perception of rural life. While the booming manufacturing cities produced wealth, they also brought unwholesome, even life-threatening, urban living conditions. Land values rose, prompting private transit companies to run car lines to suburban areas where, as the real estate brochures trumpeted, people could live in the restorative countryside with no loss of convenient access to the work place.

Andrew Jackson Downing, the undoubted, mid-nineteenth-century authority on country dwellings stated in his book, *The Architecture of Country Houses,* published in 1850:

> What we mean by a cottage, in this country, is a dwelling of small size, intended for the occupation of a family, either wholly managing the household cares itself, or, at the most, with the assistance of one or two servants. The majority of cottages in this country are occupied, not by tenants, dependents, or serfs, as in many parts of Europe, but by industrious mechanics and working men, the bone and sinew of the land, who own the ground upon which they stand, build them for their own use, and arrange them to satisfy their own peculiar wants and gratify their own tastes.

The ideal of the stalwart working-class citizen, owner of home and land, originated in Thomas Jefferson's concept of the republic founded on freeholders, or gentleman farmers, who formed a class below the gentry. According to Downing, the farmhouse—occupied by those who tilled the soil for their livelihood—was not to be confused with the cottage, "an economical little home in the suburbs of a town." Downing

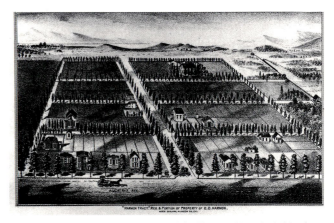

The Harmon Tract in Oakland as drawn in a lithograph from Thompson and West's 1878 *New Historical Atlas of Alameda County, California* shows a typical suburban tract from the real estate boom initiated by the arrival of the transcontinental railroad in 1868. The division of large parcels of land by their owners into small, saleable lots created varied streetscapes. Mr. E. D. Harmon's residence— with its own stand of trees— occupies the large lot at the back of the tract. Several cottages have been built on the main street.

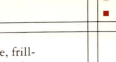

With its Gothicky ornament on the roof and the porch balustrade and railing and its Greek revival symmetry and use of quoins on the corners, this cottage marries the two most popular nineteenth-century revival styles.

Elaborate though it may seem, this is a cottage design by Newsom and Newsom that shows how the Gothic and Greek revival style elements have been elaborated to meet rising incomes and expectations.

— Front-Elevation —

Although not built on a hillside, this boxlike cottage with its main floor raised high off the ground is "nestlike," to use Stoddard's words, and lavishly landscaped. The site is probably in North Beach.

insisted that cottage design be truthful to the simple, frill-less character of cottage life. He abhorred the imitation in "cheap and flimsy materials . . . of the style and elaborate orna-ment of the villa," built for the man of "easy income." A notorious snob, Downing considered it only honest to express social status through building appearance.

Easier said than done. The wonderful new tools invented to work wood as elaborately as, but faster than, human hands could made it possible for the working man to afford an approximation of the architectural embellishments of the rich man's villa. The mid-nineteenth century was not a time when people voluntarily embraced the "simple life," as the middle class was later to do; certainly not in California, which promised fulfillment of the American Dream to all comers.

The first dwellings described as cottages in the Bay Area date from the infancy of The City, as San Francisco was com-monly called after the Gold Rush. Although the Hispanic settlers built small, cheap houses, *cottage* was a term used by the Yankees. In *Men and Memories of Early San Francisco,* the authors Barry and Patton, reflecting on the haphazard quality of life in 1849–50, note the "pleasant, homelike residence" of C. V. Gillespie, "grateful to eyes becoming familiarized with board shanties, tents, and one-story, oblong, flat-roofed dwell-ings, shooting forth long, blackened, unstable stove-pipes."

Charles Warren Stoddard, who came to San Francisco as a child in 1855, reminisced about his childhood adventures and perceptions in "Old Days in El Dorado," an essay in a book called *In The Footprints of the Padres,* published in 1902. Writing about the cottages on Telegraph Hill's northern and eastern slopes, he recalled,

> The cottages were indeed nestlike: they were so small, so compact, so cozy, so overrun with vines and flower-ing foliage. Usually of one story, or of a story and a half at most, they clung to the hillside facing the water, and looked out upon its noble expanse from tiny balconies as dainty as toys. They loomed above their front yards while their backyards lorded it over their roofs. They were usually approached by ascend-ing or descending stairways, or by airy bridges that spanned little gullies where ran rivulets in the winter season.

Unfortunately, Stoddard does not describe the occupants. We are left to wonder who could live such a genteel life in proximity to the Barbary Coast and among the rough-and-ready outcasts like the Sydney Ducks who also lived on the hill. Later in the book, the descriptions become even more improbable. (Like Downing, Stoddard was forever endowing cottages with the moral attributes.)

> This house [no location is given] stood there—I think I will say sat there, it looked so perfectly resigned. It had its shaky veranda and its French windows, and was lined with canvas; for there was not a trowel full

of plaster in it. The ceiling bellied and flapped like an awning and the walls sometimes visibly heaved a sigh, but they were covered with panelled paper quite palatial in texture and design. At the windows the voluminous lace draperies were almost overpowering. Satin lambrequins were festooned with colossal cord and tassels of bullion. A plate-glass mirror as wide as the mantel reflected the Florentine gilt carving of its own elaborate frame. There were bronzes on the mantel, and tall vases of Sevres, and statuettes of bisque brilliantly tinted. There was the old-fashioned square piano in its carven case, and cabinets from China or East India; also a lacquered Japanese screen.... paintings rocked softly on the gently heaving walls. As for the velvet carpet, it was a bed of gigantic roses....

The juxtaposition of flimsiness on the exterior with luxury on the interior may be explained by the absence of a local building industry. Although many of the Gold Rush immigrants had building skills, they did not come to California to use them. By contrast, ready money prompted the purchase of imported luxuries. Not until the first rush to the mines subsided in late 1850 and men with skills returned to the city did a local construction industry develop. Before that the market was served by the importation of prefabricated houses which were shipped around the Horn by the thousands. Such structures differed from our modern methods of prefabricating building parts to be fitted together. The "frames," as they were called, were actually built and then knocked down and packaged with their parts numbered for shipping to San Francisco. Because the buildings were built twice, and labor and shipping costs were high, the imports were only profitable as long as housing was not being built with local means.

Not all of the "frames" were small. For example, Lacryma Montis, General Mariano Vallejo's Sonoma residence, was one of three frames the General imported from Boston in 1850. In the East, where country houses were often large and grand, Vallejo's home would have been a cottage; in Sonoma it was a mansion. The other two frames were sold, one to Vallejo's son-in-law, John Frisbie, who reassembled it in Benicia where it still stands, and the other to Judge Burritt, who erected it in San Francisco on the corner of Sutter and Stockton streets. In *Men and Memories of San Francisco in the Spring of 1851,* authors Barry and Patton note "the bright, new stylish residence—its nicely curtained, spotless windows, perfect roof, and finished chimneys, neat porch, veranda, paths and doorway... nestling among the cheerless sandhills, like a sweet bit of our old home spirited across the continent by fairies' wand."

By the 1870s, 80s, and 90s, cottages that rivaled Vallejo's frames were produced inexpensively from pattern book plans using milled lumber and mass-produced ornamental detail. But in times of duress such as the Gold Rush and the post-1906 earthquake period, minimal structures were prominent. And

prominent people sometimes occupied them. John C. and Jesse Fremont lived for a time in a prefabricated house of two rooms in the mainly tent settlement in San Francisco called Happy Valley. Barry and Patton suggest that for some of the city's old timers, such dwellings were more than satisfactory. Captain Charley Scholfield, for example, had a boxlike house he called a "ranch" on Post Street next to the large lot on which Alcalde Hyde's house stood.

> Here to the last he lived as they used to live in the pioneer days; his little single cot and blankets, the big China water-jar—its cover a piece of redwood with a nail in the center for a handle—the coconut-shell dipper; a demijohn under the table; clean glasses on the table, and a box of cigars on the shelf.

Neatness, resourcefulness, and self-sufficiency seem to be the attributes that equipped the captain for a contented cottage-style life.

Development of the Contra Costa or East Bay began in the 1860s. By the 1880s, a four-page spread in the *San Francisco Chronicle* extolled the attractions of Oakland in "The City of Houses. Fair Oakland's Claims for Popularity, Its Remarkable Growth." Described as reminiscent of New England, Oakland offered houses built on lots large enough for gardens devoted to "the cultivation of rare and beautiful flowers." In contrast to the East, where such plants "must be in hothouses, they here run riot in the open air." Boom times in the mid-1880s in Oakland had, according to the article, caused new houses to spring up everywhere. The great demand seems to have been for "roomy" six-room cottages. For the population of 60,000, they could not be built fast enough.

Much of the article is devoted to the outstanding possibilities for healthy living in Oakland, particularly for "a man of modest means" who, in any case, could not afford to rent or buy a house in San Francisco unless he moved far out on the streetcar lines. Fortunate Oaklanders took the ferry where they were comfortably seated rather than suspended from a strap. After draughts of "pure fresh air" and congenial talk with friends, they arrived on the San Francisco side "fresh and vigorous" for the day in the office. Evening returned them to their homes so rested after the Bay crossing that they were in fine humor for their families.

The association of cottage life with rural-suburban life remained strong so long as rural land adjacent to cities remained to be developed and to provide release from the stress of city life for its residents. But toward the end of the nineteenth century, a reaction against the prevailing elaboration in lifestyle and buildings set in, at least in the minds of the educated middle class. The "simple home," eulogized by Charles Keeler in a book of that title published in 1904, was linked to moral superiority even as the cottage had been at mid-century in Downing's writings. Plain living—no longer a necessity—and high thinking became hallmarks of civilized refinement in an American counterculture movement that reflected the Arts and Crafts Movement in Europe.

The Frisbie house in Benicia, prefabricated in New England and shipped around the Horn to General Mariano Vallejo in 1850, is astonishing for the delicacy of its lacy bargeboards and other fancy trim that came in the package with the more functional parts. Although the cost of transporting and erecting it in Benecia are not known, General Vallejo spent about $50,000—the price of a mansion— to have his packaged "frame" shipped to Sonoma and built.

Keeler inveighed against the material progress that had produced "a class of consumers who have shamelessly disenfranchized themselves from the original conception of home" and for whom home as shelter had become a dehumanized showplace for machine-made ornament. About 1900, he founded the Hillside Club in the heart of the university community of north Berkeley. The club's objectives were to build a community, physically and philosophically, on aesthetic ideals. Low, horizontal roof lines in harmony with the hills, the integration of house and garden, the use of sleeping porches, the encouragement of open air schools and handicrafts—all these were central concerns of the club members, not just agendas for summer camp.

The Keelers lived in a house that might best be described as a series of cottages strung together on the hillside above and north of the University of California campus in Berkeley. Bernard Maybeck designed the house, built in 1895. Keeler was Maybeck's first client; they shared a reverence for craftsmanship and materials, for good carpentry and joinery in buildings and furniture, and for a handcrafted look in fixtures and decorative detail. Although simplicity implied a freedom from the pretentiousness and contrived effect that tool technology had brought to architecture in the nineteenth century, it was not necessarily primitive. In the hands of the Greene brothers of Pasadena, the Craftsman ideal was executed at a level of exquisiteness that left the simple life far behind.

The 1906 earthquake and fire left an estimated 20,000 San Franciscans homeless. Army tents were put up in twenty-eight camps around the city during the first days. In the following months the tents were replaced by relief houses, 5,610 of which were built in long rows in eleven of the camps. The houses were built by local union carpenters using plans devised by the joint efforts of Golden Gate Park Superintendent John McLaren, the Department of Lands and Buildings of the San Francisco Relief Corporation, and the U.S. Army Corps of Engineers. There were three types: A had 140 square feet and cost $100; B had 252 square feet and cost $135; C offered 375 square feet for $150. Five hundred type A houses were built of studless, board-and-batten construction in redwood and fir with gable roofs through which a metal flue for a stove projected. The exteriors were painted green, and interior walls were covered with canvas, burlap, or newspapers. The stoves were used for simple cooking—meals were served in a mess hall—and for heat. The houses were variously called earthquake cottages, camp cottages, relief shacks, and were, according to one account in the *San Francisco Chronicle,* October 21, 1906, "the teeniest, cutest little dovecotes of houses one ever saw."

When their occupants moved into more spacious houses, the shacks were often hauled out to unbuilt sites in the Sunset and Richmond districts and elsewhere. Since housing has rarely been a surplus commodity, the teeny dovecotes were often enlarged and altered to make them into permanent dwellings. A common approach was to combine two or more of the shacks. As with many temporary structures, the earthquake cottages

have become permanent, if generally unrecognized, features of some city neighborhoods. Far from disdained, they are now cherished as landmarks of a historic catastrophe. Captain Charley Scholfield's tiny Gold Rush shack on Post Street, described earlier, was probably very similar.

The aftermath of the 1906 earthquake and fire intensified residential development in suburban communities all over the Bay Area. Hundreds of people had fled the city; many thought they would never dare to live there again. Miles of houses were built on speculation in the East Bay. Many were called cottages although their size belied the name. Many more were called bungalows.

Like cottage, the term *bungalow* came from England; it had been appropriated from *banggolo,* the name of a peasant hut in Bengal, and used to describe British colonists' summer homes in the hills above Bengal. With broad overhanging roofs, encircling verandas, and sliding screen walls these small houses were well suited to the hot climate. Bungalows were first built in England in the mid-nineteenth century as vacation houses. The English distinguished them from cottages by saying that, whereas a cottage was a little house in the country, the bungalow was a little country house. (One of the earliest bungalows in this country was designed by a Boston architect and built on Cape Cod as a beach house for summer use.)

Flimsy little houses, whether for vacation use or for year-round living, were not new to California. Indeed the California bungalow was considered a building type and was much written about, particularly in the *Craftsman* magazine, published from 1901 to 1916. Articles extolled the simple life of the Craftsman movement, east and west, and offered designs for bungalows in nearly every issue. Like the cottage, the bungalow had a porch, often a deep one with overscaled columns that dramatized its importance. Halls were omitted to save space; the front door opened into the living room, a departure from most nineteenth-century plans. Windows were more broad than tall, and in general the bungalow had a low-to-the-ground look enhanced by broad overhangs on roofs. Built-in furniture was characteristic of bungalows, as it had been of nineteenth-century cottages. Walls often incorporated storage cabinets for china, display pieces, and books. Benches also covered storage units. In its most highly developed form, the interior of the Craftsman bungalow received as much design attention as its exterior.

Another real estate innovation of the bungalow era was the bungalow court. A tract of land as narrow as 50 feet wide but more often 75 to 100 feet wide and extending through the block from one street to the next was built with two rows of small houses facing each other across a common. The court plan permitted developers to raise densities while allowing people to live on the ground level, a very important part of the California image. Apartment living was considered urban and unnatural. The architectural imagery of the small houses in the courts was as often English Cottage as Craftsman. The landscaping was usually managed communally and promoted a spirit of neighborliness along with the feeling of privacy from the street.

Significant infusions of cottages into the main stream of residential building have tended to accompany abnormal rather than normal times. As we have seen, the Gold Rush and the 1906 earthquake created the kind of egalitarian social situations that made living in minimal spaces seem appropriate. Some people, no matter what their means, have chosen cottage life, perhaps because other aspects of their life were directed away from the norm. The houseboat community in Sausalito on Richardson Bay exemplifies this situation.

In the 1880s, houseboats, called *arks,* were popular in the cove waters by Tiburon and Belvedere. Several survive as Ark Row in Tiburon. The contemporary houseboat community shifted to Sausalito during and after World War II, when those interested in water-oriented activities chose to live on the water. Seems simple, but, as the number of houseboats grew, the regulation of sewage, power, etc., has made houseboat dwelling a complicated endeavor. The first houseboat dwellers scavenged their structures from wartime shards, military landing-craft hulls, balloon barges, as well as abandoned ferryboats. The mixed community weighted toward craftsmen, artists, and writers expanded to include many other walks of life. To legalize their way of life, the houseboaters organized The Floating Homes Association, Inc., in 1985 and made their structures code-conforming. Concrete foundations have pretty much immobilized the houseboats; they now line up along what look like village streets or lanes. Needless to say, they lack the rustic setting of the traditional cottage, but, as we have seen, this rusticity has become a state of mind.

With this brief look at houseboats, we have completed our review of the complex associations of that evocative term *cottage life.* Perhaps the best way to interpret the expression is to say that it implies the maximum return for the minimum investment (today the minimum may just be affordable). Investment is another of those double-edged words. One assumes that the financial investment will be smaller for the minimal house, and yet the investment of time and talent may equal that of a much larger dwelling. However the argument goes, there was a Latin motto that used to be worked into colored glass panels over the doorways of cottages. *Parva sed Apta* it read—small but just right. That may be the proof of a true cottage.

Sally Woodbridge

The elaborate landscaping of this Oakland cottage, published in Thompson and West's 1878 *Historical Atlas of Alameda County,* may have been more fanciful than real, but the varied shapes and species of trees and shrubs surely belonged to the horticultural dream setting that suburban life outside of foggy San Francisco offered.

Bungalow interiors were low-ceilinged and cozy with built-in cabinets for china and books. Furniture was often heavy as if to suggest that handcrafted pieces were, of necessity, primitive.

From the late nineteenth century through the 1920s, the most popular imagery for the cottage was that of the medieval, half-timber, thatched-roof dwelling derived from English, French, and Germanic prototypes. The example was designed by J. Cather Newsom in 1894, ten years after Newsom and Newsom's less rustic cottage shown in Figure 3.

CHAPTER I

SAN FRANCISCO'S PASTORAL ENCLAVES

✚ ✚ ✚ ✚

COTTAGE ROW

Cottage Row is the official name of this quaint pedestrian alley paved with brick and lined with plum trees traversing one block between Bush and Sutter streets in San Francisco's Western Addition. The name is also commonly used to refer to the six party-wall houses that line the alley. Developed in 1882 by Colonel Charles Taylor, they were originally described as tenements intended as low-income rental housing for the servants and clerks who worked in the neighborhood. This unique and innovative land use has been accurately described as one of San Francisco's few residential walkways comparable to an English mews.

Cottage Row was carved from the center of two land parcels—one fronting on Bush Street and the other on Sutter. The cottages were built sideways on the parcel with their fronts perpendicular to the vehicular streets on either side. This configuration meant each cottage could be only about twenty feet deep with about five feet of the parcel's width being devoted to the walkway. It also effectively concealed the presence of the tenements from the street, which considering the stuffiness of Victorian society was considered desirable. The party-wall construction saved space and materials. This unique arrangement—as you will see in the pages to come—influenced contemporary architects a century later.

The name Cottage Row was chosen by Colonel Taylor but in the 1930s the walkway came to be known as Japan Street. During this time the cottages were inhabited by Japanese Americans who held an informal open market every Saturday on the Row, selling vegetables grown in their cottages' tiny back yards. Tragically, these residents were all interned during World War II and Cottage Row was subsequently regentrified. Individual ownership of the cottages came gradually between 1956 and 1967. Today, all six cottages and the Elizabethan townhouses adjacent to them on Bush Street are designated a Historic District on the National Register.

ENGLISH COUNTRYSIDE AMBIENCE

This cottage has been the home of its graphic designer owner for about fourteen years. During this time it has been meticulously shaped into a home with the ambience of a country cottage in Devonshire. The upstairs living area retains the loft floor plan originally common to all the Cottage Row

tenements. The tiny upstairs bedroom demonstrates a masterful use of space — the elevated double bed platform has closet storage beneath, a stereo system is built into a wall niche, and shelves for books and effects are located along the walls and above the entry. Everything a bedroom could need is located in this cozy space.

"*The bedroom is shiplike, it has the cozy and compact feel of the quarters of a big sailing vessel.*"

—JAMES STOCKTON

COTTAGE CHIC

This cottage is located only a few doors down from its Devonshire-like Cottage Row neighbor. It was recently renovated by architect Suzanne Greischel and exemplifies the high design level a cottage can undergo and still remain a cottage. Glass block, granite counters, metal tubular stair railings, and high-tech German-designed lighting coexist with rustic paneling, worm-eaten wood panel doors and other examples of nineteenth-century funkiness.

"The architect and I tried to create one space on each floor to get lighting from the front of the house to the back; we got away from the chopped-up Victorian house style. We didn't work with coziness but created something very modern and uncluttered."

—AUDREY SHERLOCK

FILBERT STEPS COTTAGES

The most well known of San Francisco's numerous pedestrian streets is that section of Filbert Street between Montgomery and Battery streets on the steep eastern slope of Telegraph Hill—the Filbert Steps. This pastoral enclave, which includes the cross streets Darrell Place and Napier Lane and the nearby Greenwich Steps, is dotted with cottages that are a testament to the bittersweet challenge of cottage living. Bringing home groceries or a new piece of furniture to Napier Lane is akin to that mixed-blessing experience of seeing your worst enemy drive off a cliff in your brand new car. However, I'm sure any resident of the area would say "It's worth it. I wouldn't live any place else."

Though many of the cottages of the Filbert and Greenwich steps, Darrell Place, Napier Lane enclave deserve merit in their own right, it is the Filbert Gardens that make this area such a delight to live in or visit. The gardens are located on public land in the right of way for Filbert Street—though how the city ever planned to make this slope a vehicular street is baffling. Prior to landscaping, this area was a dumping ground thirty feet deep. Grace Marchant moved to the Steps in 1950 and sought permission from the city to clear out the dump. Permission was granted and Grace Marchant began her painstaking task of landscaping the Filbert Steps—a singular effort that consumed a period of years. The Filbert Gardens are a living monument to what one person can do for a neighborhood and a city.

This board, supported by a couple of cinder blocks, forms a resting bench for neighbors and passers-by traversing the steps. Apart from its much appreciated functional value, it is symbolic of many of the true cottager's values: Keep things simple. Don't waste more money or effort than necessary to get the job done. If the context is right, just about anything can be comfortable as well as beautiful.

"*Filbert Steps, Darrell Place, Napier Lane. In appreciation of Grace Marchant for unselfish, devoted energy in the beautification of Filbert Gardens.*"

—FROM THE PLAQUE
DEDICATING THE
FILBERT GARDENS
TO GRACE MARCHANT

MACONDRAY LANE

Macondray Lane may lack the fame of the Filbert Steps, but this Russian Hill pedestrian walk with its abundant foliage and sweeping Bay views is not lacking in captivating qualities. It accesses more large homes than cottages these days but is sprinkled with several cottages for which it provides a story-book setting.

Many Bay Area devotees have tried to convey what is so special about their city. However, I think much of the mystique is revealed in this photo of a small section of Macondray Lane. One need only ask the rhetorical question "How many cities have streets like this one?" to make the point that the Bay Area is a very special place.

MACONDRAY HIDEAWAY

*L*ocated on Macondray Lane, this cottage is barely visible from the street. It rests in the backyard of an apartment building that fronts onto Union Street and is accessed by steps that descend downhill from Macondray. Rumor has it that the structure was originally built as a church for sailors around 1890, but sometime after the earthquake it became a nickelodeon movie house. From the outside the cottage is nondescript, but inside it abounds with charming funk and some outstanding examples of flea market furniture found by the current and long-time tenant, Marianne Agnew, a graphic designer and cottage-living advocate of the first order. Casement windows open out onto a side porch providing natural light for the small dining area adjacent to a tiny kitchen that is best described as a still life.

"Finding your cottage is like Goldilocks finding the chair that is just right. It wraps around you in cozy fashion and all seems right with the world."

—MARIANNE AGNEW

Cottage Life

- Writing letters in front of the fire
- Mending
- Baking bread
- Making potpourri
- Reading Wodehouse
- Drinking tea out of flowered cups
- Listening to Telemann
- Having a cat or two

Apartment Life

- Listening to your answering machine
- Going to the laundromat
- Getting takeout
- Trying to keep your plants alive
- Reading People magazine
- Drinking Pepsi from the can
- Watching MTV
- Having a goldfish . . . that dies

—Marianne Agnew

VULCAN STAIRWAY

Though San Francisco is known for its quaint pedestrian walks, many long-time residents are not familiar with just how many there are. Vulcan Stairway in Corona Heights is a walk enveloped in overgrown foliage that accesses several picturesque cottages and is not well known outside its neighborhood. Midway along Vulcan is a shingled cottage nestled behind a large palm. This house began as a four-room cabin that has since had a floor added along with large dormer windows on the top floor that look eastward to the San Francisco skyline and the Bay.

CHAPTER II

BACK
YARD
SETTINGS

✚ ✚ ✚ ✚

BACK YARD ITALIANATE

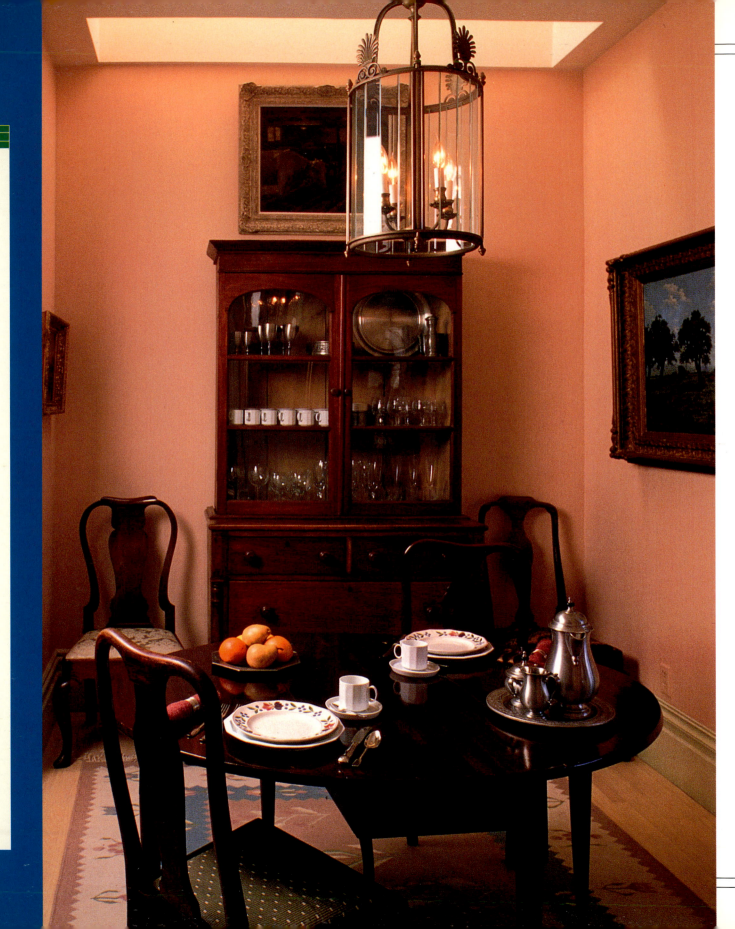

*T*his cottage is one of the most striking examples of the importance of site to the compelling nature of cottage living. The Italianate architecture of the place is replicated hundreds or thousands of times with minor variations throughout the city. (Cottages like these are referred to as "Victorian dollhouses" by the real estate community.) However, the meticulously maintained garden and the privacy of the back yard setting make this such a special place to live.

One of the city's most peculiar (and overlooked) traditions is the habit of sticking cottages behind other houses or perhaps more correctly, in some cases, the building of more substantial housing in the front yard of cottages. Whatever the scenario, these cottages are completely secluded from the street and enjoy the backyard privacy intended for the "main" house. This cottage is one of the most pristine examples of that quirky San Francisco tradition of the back yard house. It is located behind one of the Elizabethan-style townhouses on Bush Street near Cottage Row. Presumably built as rental property by Otto Esche, an early resident and owner of the main house in front, it is a classic example of a central entry Italianate cottage. Perhaps Mr. Esche was intrigued by the rental income potential on nearby Cottage Row and sought a similar situation for himself.

In the recent past, the cottage had fallen into disrepair but was thoughtfully restored by architect Richard Clayberg in the late 1970s. Skylights, a modern kitchen and bath, as well as a small V-shaped rear porch were added at this time. The basement was subsequently converted to a work/office space by the current owners, Marvin Lambert and Mary King, who needed a little more room than the 650 square feet the cottage provided.

"Living in a cottage is somewhat like living on a ship. One learns to be very creative with space and very selective about possessions. The trade-off is the uniqueness of the living experience."

—MARY KING

BACK YARD EDWARDIAN

*T*his Edwardian (well, sort of) cottage rests in the backyard of an apartment building in the Richmond district of San
Francisco. Rumor has it that the cottage was moved to the rear
of the lot so that the multiunit building could be constructed
in front. Interestingly, the chimney (assuming one existed in
the first place) was not moved with the house, rendering the
fireplace and mantel decorative elements only.

"Being in the center of the block allows us more privacy and quiet. Since we are surrounded by taller buildings we don't have a view, but we look out on our neighbors' gardens and their children at play."

—ANDREW McKINNEY

CHATCHKE HAVEN

This rented-out, back yard cottage has been embellished by a couple of long-term tenants whose passion is collecting folk art and eccentric, vernacular bric-a-brac. It is a virgin dingbat that has never been the subject of any rarefied design process. It has maintained its original character, that of a Polk Gulch farmhouse cottage. The cottage is surrounded on all sides by four-story apartment buildings. The building in front is only five or six feet from the cottage's entry porch. Sitting there contentedly, this cottage is a reminder of what a different neighborhood Polk Gulch used to be.

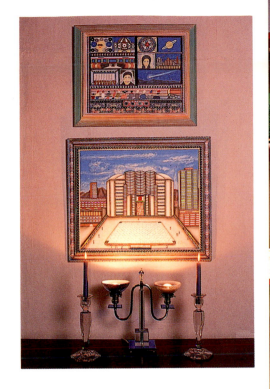

BED AND BREAKFAST COTTAGE

*T*his shingled cottage, now let as a bed and breakfast, was built around 1880 as a carriage house in the rear yard of a large Victorian but was converted to a rental unit around the turn of the century. As the "before" picture indicates, the cottage has undergone a thorough renovation by the current owner, Les Dugan, and his architect, Thomas Higley.

The side garden the cottage overlooks offers an interesting bit of San Francisco back yard intrigue. This garden, now parceled with the cottage and main house in front, was originally the back yard of the Victorian next door. At some undocumented point, the owner of the cottage property apparently convinced his unwitting neighbor to sell him the adjacent backyard—a property subdivision that is now illegal.

"Since this cottage is 'landlocked' with no automobile access, its setting gives a sense of seclusion from the urban environment and affords a feeling of uniqueness in an otherwise homogeneous architectural pattern."

—R. LESLIE DUGAN

CHAPTER III

SAN
FRANCISCO
POTPOURRI

✛ ✛ ✛ ✛

ITALIANATE RESURRECTION

From the exterior it is a typical side-entry Italianate cottage, charming though not compelling. The interior, however, is an example of the cottage form at its most quintessential. The owners, Mark and Jo Ann Coleman, both graphic designers, have used the available space creatively and populated it with collectible "stuff." Like many first-time owners they did all the renovating themselves on a limited budget. The floors, for instance, were simply stripped down to the subflooring and stained. Patches, incongruous carpentry and patina are unabashedly displayed.

The living area is a particularly fine example of the coziness that cottage scale provides. Though there is ample room for several people to sit and socialize, the room is only about 65 square feet — smaller than a typical bedroom.

"For us cottage living was one of the few options available as first time buyers. We wanted to continue to live in the City, but not in a neighborhood on the outskirts of town. We quickly learned that given this criterion, small translated to affordable.

"Though the house was small, the rooms flowed gracefully into one another. Because of the diminutive scale renovation never seemed that overwhelming. The cottage's informal, rustic character enabled us to get away with simple, naive treatments that did not require much technical skill, but rather made use of our creative energy."

—MARK AND JO ANN
COLEMAN

"The hallmark of a cottage, both literally and figuratively, is its coziness. The trick is to let the small rooms hold you in their arms, not smother you. With some renovation, this house has given me room and coziness."

—RICHARD ANDREWS

Corona Heights Cottage

This 1910 cottage in the Corona Heights area of San Francisco is the setting for an extensive renovation by architect John Walsh. A glass-roofed living area with an adjacent kitchen was added to the back and affords dramatic views of the city from both rooms. The glass roof preserves the view for a small bedroom balcony that overlooks the living room. Also, an open light well on the west side of the house was enclosed. This allows casement windows to open out on a much more gratifying space because it removes the clutter and claustrophobia normally associated with light wells.

RUSSIAN HILL PERCH

This narrow but lengthy cottage sits perched atop the western slope of Russian Hill—a site that affords a view of Nob Hill from the front room and the Golden Gate from the rear. A primitive hilavator—essentially a chair attached to a monorail—made hill climbing less of a chore (though it is currently nonfunctional).

GARDEN COURT

*O*ne of the most thoughtful complements to a tiny enclosed space is to allow it to open out visually or physically onto the outdoors. This technique is effectively implemented with the court layout so frequently associated with cottages and bungalows. Such is the case here with a reposeful garden embracing an otherwise rather nondescript court of four or five cottages on Russian Hill.

DOGPATCH COTTAGES

Dogpatch, a little-known area below Potrero Hill bounded by a freeway to the east and the industrial waterfront to the west, features an enclave of cottages on Tennessee Street. These "working-class" cottages are about twelve feet wide—only half the "narrow" San Francisco rowhouse standard.

PHOENIX COTTAGE

*A*s the sign in the window of this cottage near Mission Dolores proudly boasts, it dates from 1852, a vintage that establishes it as one of the oldest cottages in the city.

Noe Valley Cottages

This Italianate cottage in Noe Valley features some distinctive Bay Area elements—a tree fern by the front door and a picket fence careening downhill.

This Noe Valley cottage has been updated with a screening wall that provides a central entry with flanking trellis designs. The scheme allows additional privacy from the street, particularly for the lower level, while enhancing the ambience of the cottage.

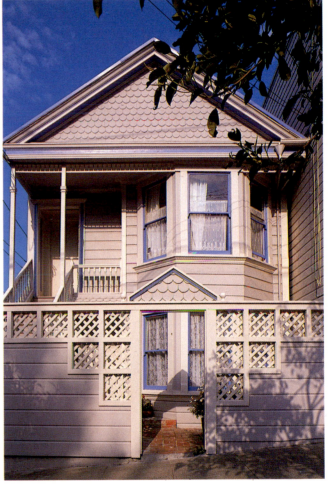

MISSION DINGBAT

*T*his cottage in the Mission is a great example of the characteristics that give rise to the oft-used term *dingbat.* Notice the peculiar alignment of the door and the ornament on the parapet in which some Italianate elements are wedded to others that defy description. On a traditional house these architectural properties would be dreadful, but on a cottage they are lovable, zany, and endearing.

FAIRMOUNT COTTAGES

*T*hese two Italianate cottages sit adjacent to one another in the Fairmount district. Their tiny front yards are overgrown with lush foliage, embracing the architecture of the houses in a satisfying way.

ITALIANATE DOLLHOUSE

*T*his Italianate cottage is a perfect complement to the acacia trees it sits behind. Its corner site shows how small its layout, and that of countless other Italianate cottages in the city, really is. The house is the same approximate depth as its width. With a central hall accessing all rooms, a typical layout accommodates four or five symmetrical rooms—500 to 750 square feet—a tiny scale that gives the term *dollhouse* specific meaning.

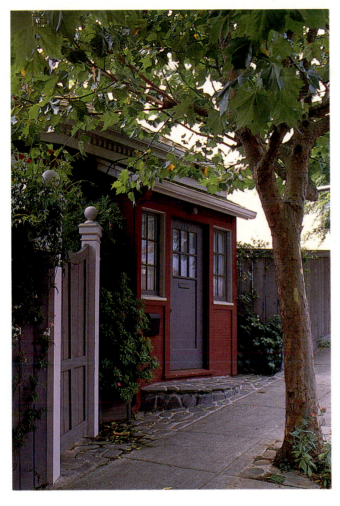

GLEN PARK COTTAGES

These cottages, like many other nineteenth- and early twentieth-century cottages in the Glen Park area of San Francisco, evoke a rural farmhouse atmosphere. They have been infilled in more recent years by housing with a more urban style, but they are a reminder that this area was once a sparsely populated pastoral hillside near the city.

BERNAL HEIGHTS

More so than perhaps any other San Francisco neighborhood, Bernal Heights evokes the shantytown atmosphere intrinsic to San Francisco in the days of the Gold Rush. This was the neighborhood where the working-class poor of nineteenth-century San Francisco lived and where some of the most substandard housing was built. Bernal's streets meander in a haphazard, careless way and are dotted with intriguing little cottages on almost every block. Rutledge Street was so named because it was originally made up of ruts in the road running along a ledge. A two-block section of Montcalm Street has no less than five surviving refugee shacks. This view of Bernal Heights is from the cottage yards of Laidley Street in the Fairmount—a neighborhood that shares a strong kindred spirit with Bernal.

MONTCALM COTTAGE

*T*his charming little box of a house sits on the downhill slope of Montcalm overlooking the city, where it is not visible from the street. Its cupola provides an appropriate crowning touch.

CONNIE'S HOLLADAY INN

*T*his cottage on Holladay overlooks the Alemany Maze and the industrial waterfront eastward. Its yard and the vacant lot next door abound with capricious funk art and a sign by the front door proudly proclaims this Edwardian cottage as "Connie's Holladay Inn." The naming of cottages is, I think, one of the most genuine evidences of the affection that cottagers feel for their homes.

CHAPTER IV

REFUGEE
SHACKS

The year 1906 still lingers in the collective memory of the Bay Area. Just as the discovery of gold in the Sierras cataclysmically changed San Francisco, so did the big quake and the ensuing firestorm. As a solution to the homeless problem created by the quake, the city built thousands of simple cottages to provide shelter until quake victims could get back on their feet. These houses were so small and basic that to call them cottages would be flattery. They are more appropriately referred to as shacks, with *refugee shack* being the preferred contemporary terminology, though *earthquake cottage* is also commonly used.

"The refugee shacks are the last tangible records of perhaps the most important thing that ever happened in San Francisco."

—DELL UPTON, UC BERKELEY PROFESSOR AND SPECIALIST IN VERNACULAR ARCHITECTURE

The shacks were looked on with disdain for they occupied—some would say scarred—prime San Francisco park lands. It was considered a social stigma to have to live in one. Local residents fought tooth and nail to keep them out of their neighborhoods. By mid-1907 the shack camps were beginning to disperse and the refugee shacks were hauled to private parcels by horse teams. Most were ultimately torn down, fell down, burned down, or were victims of miscellaneous demise (which included being cut for kindling in the camps). However, a few have managed to survive to the present. They've been modified in countless ways, as you'll see, but somewhere underneath their embellishments sits a simple board-and-batten refugee shack as tiny as 140 square feet that has survived about eighty years longer than was ever intended.

Virtually every tiny neighborhood dingbat in San Francisco is rumored to be a refugee shack, though few actually are. The confusion arises probably because there were countless thousands of small privately built cottages thrown up in 1906 to provide shelter until something better could be had. Those left homeless by the big quake who had the means built their own shacks without relying on the local authorities to do it for them. In many cases they were situated on the back of the lot so that a permanent house could be constructed in front, a scenario that created a back yard cottage once the front house was built. Like their government-constructed relatives, many of these privately built temporary cottages have survived.

Behind the Presidio Army Museum sit two type A shacks, on display to remind us all of what life in the refugee shacks was really like. These are pleasant-looking little hovels, their forest green color blending in with the park lands where they were originally located. The interiors are meager but have the rustic, frontier ambience of the miner's shacks that dotted the Sierra foothills more than fifty years before the big quake.

SUNSET SHACK

This picturesque shack is located on a sandy lot out in the avenues near Golden Gate Park. (Many refugee shacks are found near the sites of the camps—Camp Richmond in this case, now Park Presidio Boulevard. It must have been desirable not to have to haul them too far, though one enterprising individual managed to move two refugee shacks to Santa Cruz, where they still stand.) The front house consists of three shacks joined together. Its cheery red and white paint contrasts dramatically with the omnipresent ocean fog. The cobblestone fence adds an appropriate small-town ambience. In back is a free-standing type B shack which, apart from a small addition and bay window, is more or less in its original state.

In the recent past these cottages were rented out to Jane Cryan. While living here she was told by a neighborhood gadabout that the house was a refugee shack. Intrigued to no end by this information, she began to do research. Cryan discovered that her neighbor was correct and went on to found The Society for the Preservation and Appreciation of San Francisco Refugee Shacks. Her ceaseless interest in the refugee shack story has yielded many accomplishments: the documentation of over sixty shack sites to date throughout the city, a major role in the creation of the Presidio Army Museum's shack exhibit, landmark status for this shack site, and plans for a book on the definitive history of refugee shacks.

"The refugee shacks are monuments to us all— to the past efforts to rebuild San Francisco. I hope that they will stand forever as a testament to the courage of the 20,000 survivors of the great earthquake and fire who lived in them. I believe in these diminutive symbols of man's charity to his fellow man and their right to exist in our modern world.

"To live in a shack, I feel, is to be completely connected and in tune with brick, board, earth and one's neighborhood. I cleaned, patched, puttied, sawed, painted, pruned and even prayed over every square inch of the property. My two years as a shack dweller were the most idyllic years of my life. Every day I thanked fate for sending me there. I still do."

—JANE CRYAN

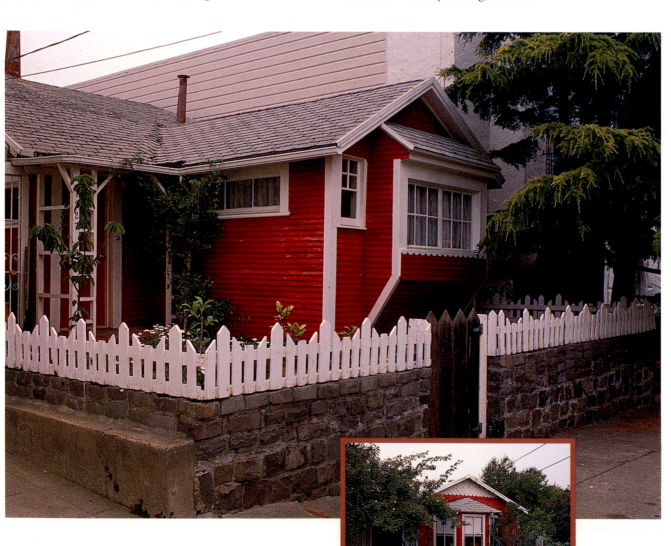

Upscale Shack

This type B shack with its french doors draped with bougainvillea, period ornament and contemporary deck would easily win the contest for most gussied up refugee shack in the city. It is now larger than its original 252 square feet and has been remodeled inside. Architect and neighbor Glenn Lym gives it high praise for its excellent siting, which takes full advantage of sunlight, panoramic view, and maximum south garden exposure. An ironic compliment, since the shack was moved here and plopped down on the flattest spot available to minimize expensive site work on the steeply sloped lot.

"I bought this house for its character. Also, I felt that even a small house like this one with its own land is more desirable than a larger, more exotic condo."

—*Dana Rich*

IMPOSTOR SHACK

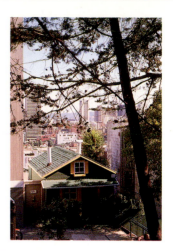

This presumed refugee shack on Telegraph Hill Boulevard is perhaps the city's most famous. It is quite ironic that extensive research compelled by impending efforts for its demolition have revealed that it is, in all likelihood, not a refugee shack after all. Non-conforming rafter construction and overall dimensions that are longer than a type A shack make a strong case that this one was a privately built cottage constructed on-site (without a building permit) sometime between 1899 and 1913. These revelations are quite an historical embarrassment as numerous books and media articles over the years have prominently featured this rustic cottage as a type A refugee shack.

For the past thirty years this humble structure has been home to Bill Bailey, retired longshoreman, union organizer, veteran of the Spanish Civil War, and renowned left-wing advocate. Bill moved here because it was convenient—he could walk to work down the Filbert Steps to San Francisco's waterfront. The walls are now covered with a lifetime of memorabilia; his lampshade bears the symbols of thirty years of political causes.

The ramped sidewalk and narrow overhang on the front remain from the days when the cottage served as an auto garage. Curiously, a former tenant placed a sash under the peak of the gable. Since it was nailed across the siding it neither opens nor lets in light—it just adds that quirky charm that all cottages need. Though probably not a refugee shack, this charming little cottage is an important Telegraph Hill landmark. It is a survivor of the raffish and bohemian neighborhood of San Francisco lore and home to a local legend.

"I think living in a little shack requires you to maintain a disciplined lifestyle. That is, there is just so much room for so much stuff. If it don't fit right, you don't buy it. As an ex-seaman used to living in cramped quarters aboard ship, this small amount of space did not change my lifestyle much.

"One great advantage of a little shack is that you don't have to go far for any convenience in the house—it's there within arm reach or leg reach. When it's rainy, cold, or windy, and you're tightly snug and warm in your little shack, life seems bearable and you feel sorta sorry for all those rich people with a dozen rooms who have to do all that worrying."

—BILL BAILEY

BONUS PLAN COTTAGE

*T*he wealthy relation of the refugee shack was the bonus plan cottage. They were actually proposed by San Francisco's mayor before the advent of the refugee shacks, but the price tag of $1,000 for the cottage and $1,000 for the lot on which to build proved unworkable for most refugee families. However, for those refugees who owned or leased land and were fortunate enough to be employed, they proved to be an alternative to living in the camps. The Department of Lands and Buildings provided the plans—designed originally by well-known San Francisco architect Bruce Porter and subsequently modified by an unknown architect to make them less expensive—and put up one-half the construction cost for them. Eight hundred eighy-five were built. The first one was located in Union Square where it was displayed to inspire refugees to participate in the program.

This bonus plan cottage on Cumberland Street has been embellished with a picket fence and cobblestone-rimmed pool in the front yard. Down the street is an interesting site that includes both type A and B shacks.

CHAPTER V

FLOATING COTTAGES

✚ ✚ ✚ ✚

FLOATING COTTAGES

Note the striking similarity in effect between these docks at Waldo Point Harbor in Sausalito and the pedestrian walks of San Francisco, particularly the Filbert Steps. They share many common elements: a walk made of wood instead of concrete and asphalt, a penchant for dressing up the walkway with castaway objects and a handcrafted, primitive look to the walkway and the cottages along it.

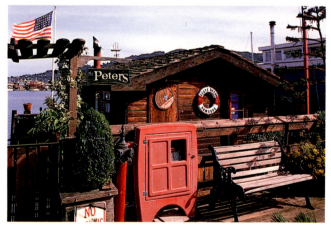

It might seem a divergence to consider the structures that we commonly call houseboats as cottages or that their existence has anything to do with the concept of cottage living. However, most of these floating structures are not boats at all. They are correctly termed *floating homes.* Being non-navigable, they are neither sea nor Bay worthy. They are typically constructed on land and transferred to a berth where they have permanent connections to city services for water and sewer, gas, and electricity—even cable TV. The only difference between these "cottages" and others included here is that these are water, rather than land, based.

The houseboat community developed in Sausalito and other parts of the Bay Area for the same reason that we find cottages located on remote hilly slopes, back alleys, in the back yards of other houses, on pedestrian walks, and other nontraditional locations. The lack of good, flat building land forced people to be creative and adopt unusual methods of land—or, in this case, waterfront—use. The floating home dwellers and the cottage dwellers of the Bay Area share the same raison d'etre, the same bohemian tradition, the same need to use interior space creatively, and, most important, the same desire to use neglected parcels to create an intriguing place to call home.

AQUATIC LODGING

Like the Lonestar, on the next page, this house was built on a landing-craft hull and was an anchor-out (one of the illegal ones) when the current owner, Ginger Harmon, acquired it in 1978. It was gradually renovated over an 8 year period and transferred to a concrete hull. With its wooden shingles and redwood trellises, it has a very distinctive cottage flair. The upper level has a bedroom with a view of Sausalito and an adjacent workspace.

"I call it my pied-à-mer."

—GINGER HARMON

LONESTAR

T his houseboat is converted, like many others, from a landing-craft hull originally built in the 1940s in Louisiana to bring ashore troops and equipment during World War II. Though it's only a single-room dwelling, it has all the essentials, including kitchen and bath facilities—even a small hot tub. Curtains are placed strategically in the space and can be drawn when privacy is needed. Casement windows on all sides open out to the Bay breeze and flood the place with light. Structural headers in the hull double as storage shelves for odds and ends.

The current owners, Michael Burt and Colleen Butler, use it as a second home for weekend and holiday getaways and informally rent it out as a bed and breakfast.

"The beauty of the Lonestar is its simplicity. Life here is wholly uncomplicated because space constraints do not permit the chaotic clutter that tends to surround us in a larger home."

—COLLEEN BUTLER

ARARAT

*I*n 1977 Stephen and Nancy Frisch bought this floating home which, at that time, consisted of a couple of leaky, drafty geodesic domes on a landing-craft hull. They lived in it for a year while planning the remodel that ultimately became a complete replacement of the old boat. Their new boat has a scale and appearance consistent with the arks—the first houseboats on San Francisco Bay (now Ark Row in Tiburon). In 1979 they orchestrated a water transfer of their boat to a new concrete hull and then spent the following four summers completing the remodel. They did most of the work themselves using recycled lumber. When their son, Noah, was born in 1984 they decided it only fitting to name the boat Ararat.

The roof of the sleeping loft opens to provide outdoor sleeping during balmy weather—a similar concept to the open sleeping porches common to turn-of-the-century Berkeley houses. Copper pipe was modified to provide supports for stair treads and has the additional benefit of allowing light and sightlines to pass through.

"Three of us, two adults and a four-year-old child live here. Although the interior physical space is small by land-based standards, it is more than compensated for by the exterior visual space. We have never felt cramped. We're a family that likes being together, so the physical closeness is natural to us."

—STEPHEN AND NANCY FRISCH

FLOATING CEDAR COTTAGE

Photographer Dennis Bayer designed this house for himself and his wife Aggie in 1985. Rather than adhering to a nautical theme, he opted for a cottage look with a double gabled roof and western red cedar siding. The overall effect is that of a floating cottage. In keeping with Far Eastern tradition, you must leave your shoes at the doorstep on entering.

"Living here is like 'getting away' every day. We fish from our deck and have become very attuned to the moon phases and tide changes. The view of Mount Tamalpais is beautiful. There is a genuine community feeling here. We can't think of any place in the Bay Area we would rather live."

—DENNIS AND AGGIE BAYER

FLOATING CABOOSE

This Sausalito houseboat is literally a caboose floating on pontoons. The observation tower is now a sleeping loft accessed by vertical stairs. The interior of the caboose contains the kitchen, dining, and living quarters. A den has been added to the rear using non-railroad components. It's a great example of how motivated individuals, like Edmund Davis who converted this caboose in the late 1970s, can find interesting alternative uses for things: former railcars and streetcars among other relics are found throughout the houseboat community. It's an interesting parallel to Carville, a community of shelters fashioned from abandoned streetcars once located on California Street near Ocean Beach in San Francisco. (Though in the case of Carville the motivation for reuse was driven by necessity rather than infatuation.)

"I chose to live here primarily because of the setting. I'm only minutes from the metropolis, but light years away in spirit. The caboose lends a certain magic, evoking images of life on the rails. No ghosts though. I think they drowned."

—*TED BARONE*

CHAPTER VI

OFF
THE
BEATEN
PATH

✚ ✚ ✚ ✚

CABIN IN THE REDWOODS

Nestled beneath towering redwoods, this cottage is one of the older structures in Mill Valley. It is located near the train station that once provided service to Mt. Tamalpais. Though it has retained much of the turn-of-the-century flavor typical of Mill Valley cabins of that era, the interior has been reworked to incorporate a loft bedroom and a modern kitchen and bath. Numerous skylights let in filtered sunlight, giving the cottage its soft glow. A rustic guest cottage in the backyard was converted from a barn that stabled the original owner's horse.

*"Cottage Life =
Organization. Our
home has very little
space, however, it has
everything a home
should have. We tend
not to hold onto junk or
things we don't like. We
love our cottage, it loves
us, and I think, at least
from what others say,
it shows."*

—LOU AND LORI SCALISE

SAUSALITO CLIFFHANGER

*T*his is a former Sausalito hillside dingbat that had brown shiplap siding and a style best described as Early Bastard. It was renovated in classic Bay Region tradition with cedar shingle siding and black trim by architect Thomas Caulfield. A new dining area was created by adding to the back of the cottage. It opens to a spacious deck with panoramic views of the Bay— a design that optimizes the informal, very livable style that cottages frequently offer.

BURBANK STREET BUNGALOWS

*I*n the heart of Alameda off Park Street is an intact block of California bungalows. Lined with tall palms towering over low-slung bungalows, Burbank Street is a journey through California's past. A walk down Burbank Street evokes the ambience of the teens and recalls the arts and crafts movement, *Craftsman* magazine, Stickley furniture, and all the other trappings of the California bungalow.

MARION COURT

*T*his tiny bungalow unit on Marion Court in Alameda and the Cadillac El Dorado out front make for an interesting scale juxtaposition. A testament to how much a house can shrink and how bloated a car can become.

STONELEIGH COURT

*T*hough courts are not that common in the Bay Area, they can be found in Alameda. Two of the most pristine of Alameda's courts are the twin courts of Stonehenge and Stoneleigh—a more bourgeois example of the "Hansel and Gretel" styles so prevalent in Berkeley in the 1920's.

Queen Anne Cottage

Much like a seven-year-old dressed up in her mother's evening gown, this Queen Anne cottage in Alameda is typical of its genre. Though the scale of this house is now considered larger than what we think of as a cottage, it was very much a cottage in the nineteenth century. Usually the basement and attic were not finished off as living, or even storage, space. The main floor accommodated about six rooms and was considered adequate for a single individual or a married couple and a single live-in servant. Its cottage status becomes quite obvious when it is compared to the scale of a typical Queen Anne house, which could easily be three times this size.

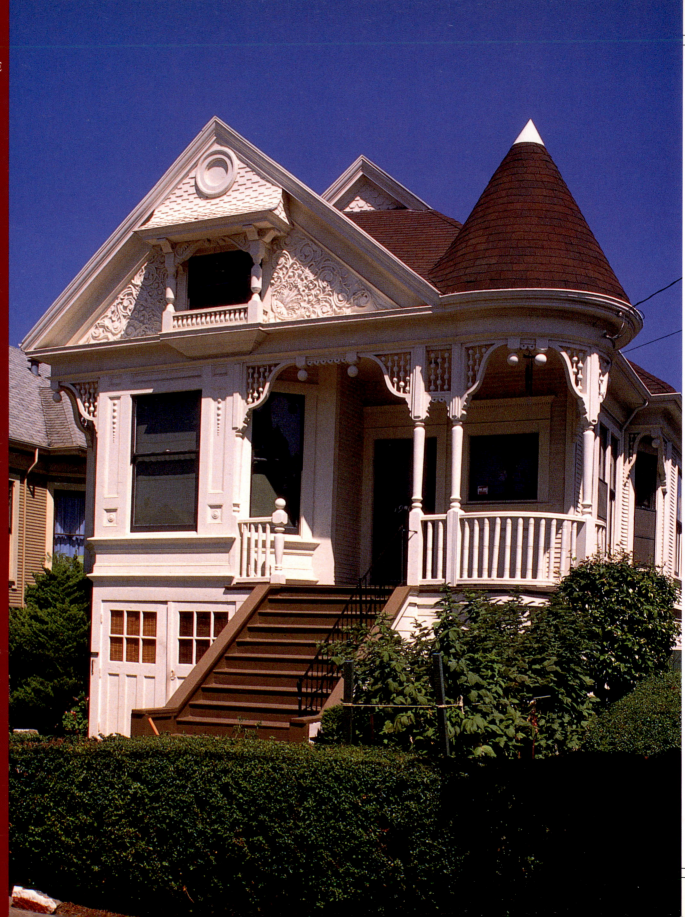

Alameda Farmhouse

*T*his cottage is typical of the early houses built in Alameda when this area was largely orchards and farmland. It is very similar to numerous cottages depicted in early atlases of Alameda County.

BENICIA COTTAGES

*B*enicia is the town time forgot. This small town at the mouth of the Sacramento delta was the first capital of California, but somehow the boom times that catapulted California forward passed it by. The streets of old Benicia are lined with nineteenth-century cottages —much like these—interspersed with historical landmarks of California's early days.

CHAPTER VII

BERKELEY'S
PURSUIT
OF
COTTAGE
UTOPIA

✚ ✚ ✚ ✚

I n turn-of-the-century San Francisco, living in hillside cottages was largely relegated to the poor and outcasts, but in Berkeley, hillside living was an intellectual pursuit. Charles Keeler was the chief spokesman and Bernard Maybeck the principal architect of this movement. Across the Bay wealthy San Franciscans had been building ostentatious mansions that were much despised by Berkeley bohemians, who favored houses that included vernacular, arts and crafts elements, and had a hand-crafted look—traits we closely associate with cottages. Keeler extolled his housing philosophies in his book *The Simple Home,* which became a manifesto for Berkeley hillside living. Many Berkeley hillside homes that adhered to Keeler's philosophies are cottages in style only, since they are larger than homes we now think of as cottages. Some are quintessential cottages both in style and scale.

This house is just such a place. Designed by Maybeck in 1902, it is adjacent to Keeler's home, which Maybeck designed as his first private commission in 1895. With its steep gable, organic shingles, and siting that optimizes the garden and view, the Keeler studio is a consummate hillside cottage reflecting the simple home concept.

"Hillside architecture is landscape gardening around a few rooms for use in case of rain."

—FROM *THE HILLSIDE CLUB BULLETIN, CHARLES KEELER, PRESIDENT 1903–05*

MATHEWSON COTTAGE

Maybeck understood the extraordinary importance of site to his architecture—which is why he bought large areas of land in the Berkeley hills on the north side of the University of California campus. He paid very little for this land because, as in San Francisco, the most sought-after land was in the flatlands near services and the waterfront. Maybeck realized that eventually the hillsides, with their dramatic views, exuberant foliage, and secluded sites, would be desirable.

This small house is located in those now-desirable hills north of the Berkeley campus, just across the street from Maybeck's house (which burned down in the Berkeley fire of 1923). Maybeck designed this cottage for R. H. Mathewson in 1915. He met the challenge of a limited budget by creating a small scale house with simple carpentry details. The cottage has no formal dining room, which saves space, and the living area is an open loft that feels spacious beyond its actual square footage. The exterior use of color is remarkably contemporary with gray-green stain on the board-and-batten siding and aqua-colored window mullions. The low, overhanging eaves give the cottage a tight harmony with its pastoral setting.

The Mathewson cottage is certainly one of Maybeck's greatest houses. The small scale contributes greatly to its success. Maybeck's appreciation for simple, earthy elements in his houses is fully realized when applied to cottage scale structures.

TUFTS COTTAGE

Built in 1931 in the Berkeley hills, this was the third house Maybeck designed for J. B. Tufts—the other two had been in Marin County. Despite the fact that he had the means, Tufts did not require a large house as he lived alone and the house needed only to accommodate himself and a single servant.

Maybeck's special genius as a designer is revealed in the view of the east elevation of the Tufts house. In admiring its quaint "Hansel and Gretel" charm, one hardly notices that this elevation contains the doors of a two-car garage—an element required in twentieth-century homes that seldom lends any charm to the structure. The designs on the garage and entry doors were hand-painted by Maybeck. The living room features a massive, asymmetrical cast concrete fireplace.

The current owners have fashioned a garden entry inspired by English cottage gardens.

KELLOGG COTTAGE

This shingled cottage was designed by Maybeck in 1902 for UC Berkeley English professor Hiram Kellogg. It was originally located on Regent Street in Berkeley but was moved—apparently in sections—to nearby Linden Avenue. The interior of unfinished redwood creates a feeling of rusticity that is enhanced by an adjacent fig arbor, a highbacked settle near the entry, and symmetrical gabled ceilings for both of the upstairs bedrooms. A sectional view of the ceiling detail resembles an inverted W capped by a larger inverted V. This design gives a comforting sense of enclosure to each bedroom and creates a diamond shaped "attic" between the two rooms.

"Stone and wood construction bears the same relation to architecture as the piano does to the music played upon it. Architecture and music are conveyors of expression of human experience."
—BERNARD MAYBECK, 1915

WALLEN MAYBECK COTTAGE

This house was designed by Maybeck for his son Wallen and his wife Jacomena in 1933. It is a modest house with a loft living/dining area and a galley kitchen at the south end. The lower level has bedrooms and a bath. Decks on the west side of the house look out to the view of the Berkeley hills and the Bay. Late in his life Maybeck moved into this house with his son's family and lived there until he died in 1957.

To the layman, Maybeck might seem anchored in nineteenth-century traditions, but while he kept one foot there his other was firmly planted in the twenty-first century. Innovative in his use of materials, Maybeck integrated corrugated metal, cast concrete, plywood, and concrete-dipped burlap into his houses. Also, he used unfinished surfaces such as plywood (used for ceiling and walls in this cottage) in his interiors and allowed structural elements to serve as ornament long before these concepts became common. Yet, his experimentation was never counterproductive to a sense of rightness anchored in traditional, heartfelt values. His houses possess the human qualities we closely associate with cottages.

"Cottages allow you to be either formal or informal in the way you live and entertain, but they don't impose any of the rigid formality of more conventional homes.

"The cottage ideal grew up around us and became a very personal expression of the way the Maybeck family chose to live. Maybeck considered the fireplace to be the living heart of the house. Even his smallest houses had large fireplaces. It was always the gathering place for the family.

"The vernacular forms of Maybeck's houses evoke a strong sense of the past and the setting keeps one in tune with the environment — the garden, the breeze, the sun, the elements of nature."

— JACOMENA MAYBECK

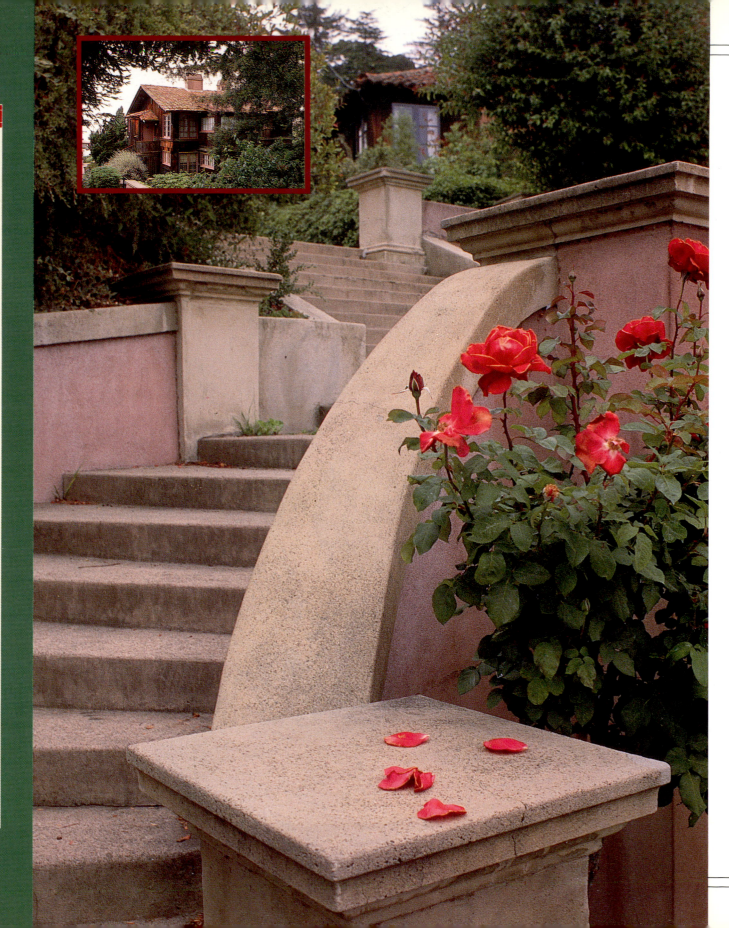

ROSE WALK

Rose Walk is a pedestrian walk designed by Maybeck in 1912 that traverses north from Euclid Avenue connecting to Rose Street one block up the hill. The cottage houses dotting the walk were designed by Henry Gutterson whose style David Gebhard has aptly described as being of "the Hansel and Gretel cottage world."

Rose Walk epitomized the town planning advocated by the Hillside Club. It makes for a striking comparison to the hillside pedestrian walks of San Francisco which evolved haphazardly rather than being the product of an intellectual design process. It is further evidence of the radical difference in approach to hillside living between the Berkeley bohemians and the working class of San Francisco, though interesting living environments were created in both situations. Proof that given a hillside with natural foliage, a sweeping view and a "simple home," it is virtually impossible to go wrong.

BERKELEY HILLS SECLUSION

This 1916 Berkeley Hills cottage is home to architect Thomas Caulfield and family. It is a very special example of architecture and site working together to produce a total cottage environment. The living areas are open to each other; separation is provided by a central fireplace/stair element. Windows on all four sides ensure a light and airy feeling and expand the small rooms. High ceilings and skylights further enhance the spacious feeling.

Views from both floors are of surrounding woods. The small scale of the house is accentuated by the 75- to 100-foot redwoods and laurels that tower over the house and provide a sense of enclosure.

The low-ceilinged study off the master bedroom is a converted open sleeping porch— a popular feature in early twentieth-century East Bay houses. Sleeping outdoors was believed to promote good health and ward off colds in the winter.

"*My mental image of cottage comes from the Disney movie* Snow White and the Seven Dwarfs. *Our house fits this image as much as real life permits. It even had a couple of "dwarfs" for ten or twelve years, but they turned into monster teenagers. We chose this house mainly for its separation from neighbors by woods. The privacy this affords is one of its greatest benefits. The frequent presence of creatures like deer, raccoons, squirrels, opossums, birds, mice, slugs, and snails reinforces the sensation of living in a forest.*

—THOMAS CAULFIELD, ARCHITECT

WURSTER TWIN COTTAGES

These two cottages were designed by William Wurster as rental property and are located across the street from his development at Greenwood Commons in Berkeley. They are a rare example of architecturally meaningful post–World War II cottage building in the Bay Area. Apart from those bungalows of the outer Sunset and similar areas that were thrown up as starter houses for returning GIs eager to resume family life, there was little local cottage building . By the late fifties cottage building in the Bay Area was virtually non-existent for the first time since before the Gold Rush. It wasn't revived until the seventies when land values and construction costs sent architects and developers scurrying to find ways to make housing more affordable.

Like the Jensen house in the Berkeley hills and the Clark house in Aptos, these cottages are one of the best examples of cottage scale architecture by one of the Bay Area's most important modern architects. Though Wurster was not known for having any specific agenda relating to cottages and cottage style, his obvious concern for rustic elements, informal, very livable layouts, and the integration of interior and exterior components of house and site was in sync with cottage traditions. Much of his work is a continuation of the ideals of "the simple home" as put forth by Keeler and Maybeck. It was this element of Wurster's work that in great part led International Style mogul Marcel Breuer to comment "if 'human' is considered identical with redwood all over the place, I am against it."

"Sheetrock is actually cheaper than Douglas fir plywood, but plywood looks cheaper, so let's use it."

—WILLIAM WURSTER

CHAPTER VIII

CONTINUING
THE
COTTAGE
TRADITION

✦ ✦ ✦ ✦

MODERNITY COMES
TO A RUSTIC ADDRESS

Located between Russian Hill and Polk Gulch on Green Street in San Francisco, this was the site of a post-earthquake cottage that for many years was the home of Imogen Cunningham. Stephen Goldstine bought the house from the Cunningham estate and initially intended to renovate and expand the historic old cottage to suit his family's needs. Rumor had it that the cottage was a refugee shack. All evidence indicated that given the date, scale, and siting of the cottage at the back of the lot, it could have been a privately built earthquake cottage but was definitely not a refugee shack. Despite the intent to save the old cottage, it was so substandard that no code-conforming chunk of it could be found to use as a building block for an updated house. The result was the razing of the old cottage and the con-struction of a new one matching the original's footprint.

The new cottage is a collaborative design by architects James Monday and Lars Lerup. Its clean, simple, and essentially mod-ern lines integrate extremely well with the site, producing a house with a cozy, cottage feeling without engaging in a literal interpretation of cottage form and element. The building is a small house with a living/kitchen/dining area below and two bedrooms above; it sits atop a workspace/dance studio with no interior passageway between the two. Masterful storage solu-tions are found throughout the house, allowing its small scale to accommodate large volumes of music, books and art as well as a home office.

From the street this lot looks like a side yard for the house next door, as the cottage in the rear is barely visible. It is this radically differing land use that makes Russian Hill such an interesting neighborhood: apartment buildings tower above tiny cottages nestled between them — a formula that current city planners demand we abandon in order to maintain a more uniform streetscape.

Laidley Castle

Laidley Castle is the first of two renovations of Laidley Street cottages by architect Jeremy Kotas. Before renovation, the small cottage on this site was a dingbat with three sheds off the street side of the house and one on the view, or back, side of the house. The central part of the cottage was held together with 4×4s at the corners with 2×4 stringers between — typical of the unorthodox, non-code-conforming construction found in old San Francisco cottages. The peak of the cottage's gable was barely visible from the street, due to its location on the downslope of a hill.

Kotas initially wanted to remodel the cottage by creating a deck at street level with an entry tower opposite, thus inspiring

the name Laidley Castle. The name stuck though the design didn't. Kotas ultimately opted for a more conventional approach to remaking the cottage, though the final version is filled with eccentricities. A common garage door conceals the unexpected—an open air dining area adjacent to the kitchen. A Buick hubcap, found at the site during renovation, adorns the wall above the kitchen sink—an element retained by the current owners Raymond and Kay Roberts. French doors in the master bedroom open out to a subterranean garden concealed from the street above by a redwood trellis that filters the light of the afternoon sun.

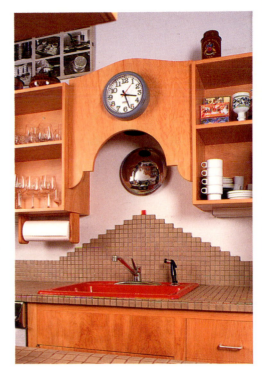

"In the ordinary sense of the word, I would never describe Laidley Castle as a cottage. However, it does have cottage elements though its scale is now larger than a typical cottage. The entire upper floor is open but has been divided into a lot of little alcoves designed so you can never see the entire floor from any point. Really, Laidley Castle is a one-room house apart from the bedrooms and baths. When you walk in the front door you are in a single room that contains everything you need for living."

—JEREMY KOTAS

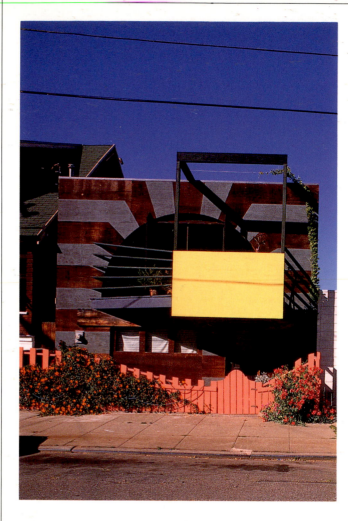

TRANSITIONAL EXPERIMENT

*H*aving sold Laidley Castle, Jeremy Kotas turned his attention to a four-room 1907 cottage just down the street where he began a second extensive cottage renovation that, in the mind of the renovator at least, remains only partially complete. The front siding consists of panels of rough finished plywood, but is embellished by an eccentric use of color inspired by primitive Mexican folk art.

Like Laidley Castle, this cottage is built around one, multi-purpose room with the master bedroom on a mezzanine above. A clever space-saving design has the bath tub set in a niche off the bedroom with toilet and lavatory in a separate room adjacent. Another feature shared with Laidley Castle is the garage door that opens to a study rather than a garage.

"This house is an elaboration of the one-room idea from Laidley Castle in that it incorporates a two story volume in its living space. I was inspired by Byzantine churches, store front studios, and the industrial warehouses downtown that had these wonderful open lofts. I call this the largest one-room house in San Francisco."

—JEREMY KOTAS

Jeremy Kotas honed his architectural skills by metamorphosing dingbat cottages on Laidley Street. Though he was not self-consciously designing within a cottage frame-work, the challenges posed by the quirkiness of those two structures led to a rapport with the cottage form that played a major role in the manner he and his partner Anthony Pantaleoni approached this recent San Francisco project. The site on California Street was a difficult infill situation—a vacant lot that was a side yard to a large Victorian Italianate. The original intent of the developer was to place a five-unit apartment building on the site—an idea which quickly proved to be unworkable. The ultimate solution became a literal update of the layout of San Francisco's Cottage Row. By placing a landscaped footpath along the west side of the site, five cottages (actually a contiguous structure that appears to be separate cottages) could be stacked, one overlooking the other, with entries along the footpath. The resemblance to Cottage Row was so striking that the project came to be referred to by that name by both developer and architect.

Some truly wonderful cottage elements were incorporated into the structure, including a blind window on the front cottage, gables that change pitches, abrupt juxtaposition of differing siding materials and window sizes, ornamented brackets beneath a window bay that are at 90 degree angles to one another, and so on. Quite deliberately, the illusion is fostered that the cottages clustered on the site were built over time with only incidental relationships between them—an insightful though somewhat satirical homage to cottage style. In keeping with the spirit of the project, Frances Butler created a whimsical mosaic in the entry niche using leftover tile from the kitchens and baths.

The cottages range from just over 500 to just under 1000 square feet and incorporate numerous space-saving devices: stairs as narrow as the code allows, sleeping lofts accessed by folding stairs, arched niches carved from beneath stairs, while bay windows add space here and there. The illusion of space is created with high-ceilinged lofts and generous use of windows.

"I never thought of these five units as cottages, but as urban bungalows. When I worked with the planning commission and was involved with the city-wide survey, we found many elements of craftsman bungalows in houses throughout the city. I wanted to incorporate those elements in this project. We made an interesting companion to the larger existing architecture by breaking our building up into pieces with cranky little details and overscale ornament."

—JEREMY KOTAS

REFINING THE AFFORDABLE HOUSE

*D*onald MacDonald is a passionate believer that the revival of the cottage residence is the best solution to affordable housing in the Bay Area. He advocates that the cottage is the most psychologically satisfying manifestation of a tiny living space that can be readily and inexpensively constructed. His newest cluster of cottages in San Francisco at Duboce and Steiner streets includes four cottages — each with a footprint of only 12 × 20 feet and containing less than 630 square feet including a one-car garage (which is actually a multiuse space that can be readily converted to a living/work space). The sleeping area appears to be suspended from the roof above the main living area though it is actually supported by a beam beneath. The walls in the tiny sleeping space are kept open to prevent claustrophobia and create an illusion that the space is larger than it actually is. Drapes or blinds can be hung to create more privacy. Even though these cottages have been designed to be as affordable as possible, they contain interesting architectural elements and complex spaces that make up for their lack of square footage with large volumes of space (the living area has over a twenty-foot ceiling height) and large windows that look out onto a park.

These were the first of MacDonald's cottages designed to get the most from the least and were inspired by a cottage drawing by his seven-year-old daughter Denise. The grid—an overlay of 1 × 4 battens painted gray—creates a simple albeit provocative ornament that evokes a craftsman theme. The layout is evocative of the interior plan of the Wallen Maybeck house in Berkeley and shares similarities to the interior layout of the Cottage Row houses. Its layout consists of an open floor plan on the second floor which accommodates living/dining and kitchen with bedrooms and bath down. A sleeping loft accessed by ladder is perched beneath the gable peak on the second floor.

CLINTON MEWS

*T*his cluster of cottages on Guerrero Street at Clinton revives the concept of the cottage court. Ten cottages fit into this tight site which maximizes the allowable density—quite a feat considering that each cottage is a separate structure only half the allowable height limit. A condominium building originally planned for the site would not have accommodated any more family units. All the cottages enjoy the added privacy of fronting a courtyard rather than the street. They are similar in layout to MacDonald's grid cottages.

COTTAGE ROW
REVISITED

*T*his row of cottages is identical to MacDonald's gridded cottages, but with a more traditional exterior siding treatment. All four cottages were sited on a single San Francisco corner lot by reviving the "sideways" configuration found on Cottage Row.

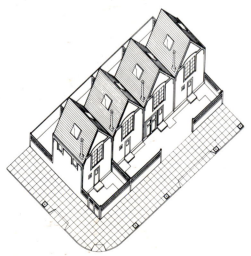

THE PAST IS TOMORROW:
The Revival of the Cottage
by Donald MacDonald

The house of moderate cost is not only America's major architectural problem but the problem most difficult for her major architects.
— FRANK LLOYD WRIGHT

The traditional symbol for a house is a square with a pitched roof. Easy to draw, it is among the first images children put to paper. Add to it a chimney, a door, one or two windows, smoke coming out of a chimney, and perhaps some flowers in front and a fence, and the picture is complete: a cottage. For what-ever reason—whether the easy rendition inspires the sentiment, or the image has primordial emotional roots—the picture of a cottage continues throughout the lives of many Americans to represent home, security, coziness, warmth, family. It also symbolizes escape. Because a cottage is simple, inexpensive, and embracing, it connotes a haven from the struggle to make a living, from harassment, from worry, from routine. Aging office workers dream of retiring to a cottage in some quiet community on a lake or roaming the country in a Winnebago motor home or other such cottages on wheels.

In the Bay Area (as elsewhere in the country), wistful senti-ment is very close to economic reality. A cottage is the only type of house an increasing number of people have any hope of owning. For young couples it is the perfect starter home—the first step on the road of fulfilling their fantasy. Properly designed and placed on a suitable lot, a cottage is as economi-cal to build and maintain as an apartment of the same square footage in a multiunit residential building. With sensible financing, monthly mortgage payments can be about the same as rent for comparable apartments in the neighborhood and less than mortgage and maintenance payments for condominiums with the same space. Cottage construction is a very feasible and very desirable way to meet the rapidly growing need for afford-able housing.

Why, then, have so few cottage-type homes been built since World War II? One answer, and probably the basic one, is that residential developers have focused on the lucrative middle-income market. In the 1950s and 1960s, when the economy was booming, the population growing, and the urban middle class fleeing to the suburbs as fast as it could, tract homes sold as quickly as they could be built and nice, new (although unimaginatively designed and poorly constructed) apartments were often rented before the building was finished. Then came the condominium and developers were so ecstatic over the rapid return on their investments that construction of rental units and moderately priced houses declined to the point that shortages occurred in many parts of the Bay Area.

By the early 1980s the need for affordable housing had become critical. But zoning laws, codes, and financing systems prevented builders from responding to the demand. Adopted primarily for middle-income construction, the standards set made it virtually impossible to build inexpensively. Lot requirements of a quarter acre or more; space, insulation, fire-resistance, and myriad other regulations; and financing based on the more complex codes and higher profit anticipation all increased the cost of construction so much that affordability was defined in effect as housing in the lower middle-income range. Under these constraints, a cottage did not cost that much less to build than a tract home.

Revival of cottage construction and consequent revitalization of the American dream of home ownership must begin with innovative architectural designs that demonstrate how costs can be reduced and that serve as guidelines for modification of codes, zoning regulations, and financing arrangements. The designs must include a cost-effective form, a realistic percep-tion of space requirements, the practical use of materials, and employment of new technologies that enable occupants to maintain their homes easily and modify them as needed.

The most economical two-dimensional shape of a building is a square. A matter of simple geometry, any deviation greatly increases the amount of materials needed, as the following example illustrates. A 400 square-foot building 20 × 20 feet in size has 80 linear feet of wall. A rectangular 400 square-foot building 10 × 40 feet has 100 linear feet of wall. The same economics apply to the vertical proportions, of course; there-fore, a cube is the ideal form of a cottage. Within these constraints a great deal of flexibility is afforded if traditional space allotments for rooms and other restrictions are modified.

Although a cottage by definition is small, it need not look or feel like a doll's house. The principal living areas can be as commodious and comfortable as those in a much larger house—indeed, more so than some of the tract homes built at much greater cost. But, of course, sacrifices have to be made in order to compensate.

As a result of the focus on middle-income housing, most architects and codes have a distorted perception of space requirements. They assume that a certain amount of space is required for each person and each activity. They hold as invio-late the requirement that ceilings in most rooms should be at

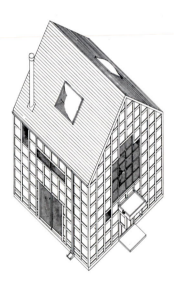

least 8 feet high—in some instances, at least 9 feet high; that bedrooms must be at least 90 square feet; and that staircases should be no steeper than 42 degrees.

But why must bedrooms have 8-foot ceilings and be at least 90 square feet? Bedrooms are to lie down in and sleep. Unless the occupant is a basketball player, there's no reason why a bedroom can't have a 7-foot ceiling, or even one 6.5 feet high. Sixty-four square feet is more than ample for a bed and dresser. If the bedroom ceiling is lower in a two-story house, the living room—where people spend time awake—can be higher. If you place the living room on the second floor and design 64-square-foot bedrooms, the garage can be incorporated into the house itself. This reduces the requisite size of the lot and thus the price of the home. In a one-story house, such smaller dimensions allow more space for other functions.

Similarly, the steeper the staircase, the more space available for other functions. Each 5 degrees of incline requires about 3 extra square feet of unoccupiable space. There's also no reason why a garage has to be only a garage or a living room only a living room, or for that matter a bedroom only a place to sleep. By incorporating the garage into the house, it can serve as a guest room, study, or playroom. Incorporation of the kitchen into the living room (as is done in many modern apartments) results in a less confined space for preparing meals and a more open feeling in the room.

In fact, functional allotments of space are not necessary at all, except for kitchen utilities and bathrooms. If the entire floor is left undivided by the architect, the people who live in the house can separate it into areas any way they want to with accordion dividers, like those used in hotel ballrooms to convert them into meeting rooms. At very little extra cost, tracks can be run across the ceiling in various places. A living room can thereby be converted into bedrooms at night, or a part can be set aside as a study. One large bedroom can be converted into two or three as needed.

Certain well-known but not always well-employed architectural techniques create an illusion of space. White paint, mirrors, and bright lighting make a room look much larger than it is, as do generous windows, although they add to the cost of construction. Glass-top tables, chairs made of metal tubing and leather or plastic, and low furniture enhance the sense of spaciousness. Carpets should be of a continuous light color. If the living room is on the ground floor, the back yard should be integrated with it by the use of french doors. A top-floor living room should certainly have a skylight.

Substantial savings are possible with the prudent use of materials. In a climate like the Bay Area's, where temperatures rarely fall below 45 degrees, the code requirements of insulated walls and dual-glazed windows to conserve energy are extravagances. Older buildings with single walls and single-glazed windows are comfortable even without heat most of the time. Air conditioning is unnecessary in San Francisco; few homes outside the city have it because the summer heat is so dry. The advantage of reduced construction costs resulting from single walls and single-glazing far outweigh the benefits of conserving a little bit of energy.

Wood is an excellent insulator and, in general, a superb construction material, both structurally and aesthetically. Plentiful on the West Coast, it is ideal for building cottages. Utilizing 2×4s, a standard component of the building industry, as much as possible throughout the building, is another way of reducing costs. Wood's greatest feature is its aesthetic value. The texture, malleability, and color afford the architect marvelous opportunities for individualized designs.

Reduced construction costs will not have an appreciable effect on the price of a cottage, however, unless zoning laws are changed. The usual minimum lot size of a quarter acre or more is fine for a house of moderate dimensions, but for a 400-square-foot structure, 800 to 1,000 square feet is ample. And the laws should permit cottages on small lots to be interspersed with larger homes as long as the designs are attractive.

Banks should bend over backwards to promote the construction and sale of such cottages, just as they did for condominiums. The potential market is enormous, and the risk involved is comparatively low. Many such cottages built in San Francisco in the 1980s sold immediately as they were built, demonstrating the intense desire of a great many people to own their own homes as well as their willingness to settle for small ones if that's what they can afford.

In the final analysis, the revival of cottage construction means a revitalization of a democratic tradition that has been rapidly expiring during the past few decades. Only the economically privileged have been able to buy homes, and with rising costs the level of this privilege has become higher and higher. The result has been the exclusion of an increasing number of people from enjoyment of one of the great benefits of a free society. Home ownership, with the comfort and security it connotes, should be achievable by everyone who wants it and works for it.

Donald MacDonald is a San Francisco–based architect and the founder of MacDonald Architects and Planners. He has been the recipient of numerous national and international design awards and has been called "the most boldly creative practitioner in all of architecture" by Architecture Dean Raymond Yeh of Oklahoma University. He holds a masters degree in architecture from Columbia University and is a Fellow in the American Institute of Architects. He is one of the nation's leading advocates and practitioners of cottage design and development as a solution to affordable home ownership.

INDEX

FOR FURTHER INTEREST...

Presidio Army Museum
Presidio of San Francisco
Hours: 10 am to 4 pm Tues. thru Sun.
Phone: 415.561.4115

The Presidio Army Museum features a refugee shack exhibit located directly behind the museum building. Two shacks are on display. One shack has a re-creation of a typical shack interior. The other has a display of refugee shack history with vintage photographs of shacks, the shack camps and other memorabilia.

The Society for the Preservation and Appreciation of San Francisco Refugee Shacks
Phone: 415.759.6429, leave message

Jane Cryan, the Society's founder, is the definitive authority on San Francisco Refugee Shacks. She is actively involved in documenting shack sites throughout the City and intermittently offers tours and lectures on the subject.

The following cottages/floating homes are let as bed & breakfast accomodations. Information regarding rates and availability can be obtained from the individuals listed.

Lonestar, Sausalito, pages 68–69
Coleen Butler
Lonestar Houseboat
South Forty Pier
Berth 41
Sausalito, CA 94965
415.433.3348

Bed & Breakfast Cottage, San Francisco, page 36
R. Leslie Dugan
2548 Pine Street
San Francisco, CA 94115

Bed & Breakfast Cottage, San Francisco, not shown
Ruth Potter
2446 Washington St.
San Francisco, CA 94115
415.922.0346

THIS BOOK WAS
COMPOSED IN GARAMOND NO. 3 BY
ON LINE TYPOGRAPHY,
SAN FRANCISCO

IT WAS PRINTED
AND BOUND BY
DAI NIPPON PRINTING CO., LTD.
TOKYO, JAPAN

DESIGN & PRODUCTION BY
THOMAS INGALLS + ASSOCIATES,
SAN FRANCISCO